The Shadow World © 2023 Caity Randall & Craig Ford.
All Rights Reserved.

No part of this book may be reproduced in any form or by any electronic or mechanical means including information storage and retrieval systems, without permission in writing from the author. The only exception is by a reviewer, who may quote short excerpts in a review.

This is a work of non-fiction. The events and conversations in this book have been set down to the best of the author's ability, although some names and details may have been changed to protect the privacy of individuals. Every effort has been made to trace or contact all copyright holders. The publishers will be pleased to make good any omissions or rectify any mistakes brought to their attention at the earliest opportunity.

Cover illustration by Michelle Webb
Internal illustrations by M. K. Perring

Printed in Australia
First Printing: May 2023

Paperback ISBN 978-1-7637569-9-1
Hardcover ISBN 978-1-7637570-2-8
eBook ISBN 978-1-7637570-0-4
Audiobook ISBN 978-1-7637570-1-1

Cyber Unicorns
www.cyberunicorns.com.au

 A catalogue record for this book is available from the National Library of Australia

CAITY RANDALL & CRAIG FORD

Introduction

This book is very different from what you may have read before. It will teach you about a dangerous place that you may or may not be aware of – a world containing a lot of shadows.

Much like real life, there are many shadows where you can't see who, or what, is in them when using your computers, on the internet, gaming and much more. Shadows can be scary! But we are here to show you that much like the shadows you see in your home, these aren't so scary when you turn a light on. Once you learn how to shine your **knowledge torch** on these internet shadows, you will see lots of ways to protect yourself, and others, from this shadow world – which isn't so scary once you know what you're looking at.

The topics we will introduce you to may not

mean anything yet. They may be concerning, or even a little frightening but if that is the case, we encourage you to start a conversation with your class, or with a trusted adult to help you be more comfortable with them. This is the main idea for this book. It is not to teach you everything you need to know but to arm you with your first torch to shine on these shadows, even to ask more questions and to learn more about being safer in the digital world we all engage in. As you get older, you will use technology more and this book is designed at helping you gain a better understanding of the shadows you face along your journey.

This book will transport you on a quest to being smarter online and is one filled with stories and adventures as you read and learn. You will be able to pick any chapter you want from the book to gain knowledge of specific topics to help you deal with any problem you may face. You can read it front to back in order, or flick around chapters as you please!

We are here to help you learn about what is hiding in this shadow world, so should you ever come across one of these scary shadows, you will know that your knowledge torch can shine a light on them and make that shadow disappear.

Now, let's get into some adventures and get your torches ready for action!

What Is This Internet Thing Everyone Talks About?

We live in a big, beautiful world with a lot of different big cities, small towns, outback areas and interesting things to see. Just like the Earth, we can think of the internet as a big place where knowledge from all over the world is stored, shared and created. There are so many cool things to see on it!

We can use the internet to watch a rocket launch into space; we can watch lion cubs on video streams; we can buy food to be delivered to our door; we can learn about a vast number of things and even play fun games with our friends – and so much more!

The internet is a virtual world and was created before many of you were born. If we think of it in the simplest way, it is millions of computers that are all connected and sharing information.

To make things easy on the internet, we can use search engines to find the things we seek or need, like superheroes, or cute horse videos. It is an amazing space that can help us solve problems or talk to loved ones without being in the same house, city, or even country!

However, the internet is not all fairy floss and rainbows. There are scary things that you need to learn to look out for, like how you learnt to cross the road, or check the ground for snakes and spiders when on a bushwalk. Once you know what to look for and what things you can do to keep safe from these dangers, you will become stronger and you can make the most of the whole wide world that is now at your fingertips through the world wide web.

The first thing you need to learn about being online is that not everything, or everyone, who you may meet and see is often real. Bad people may try to trick you into things online, like buying something that doesn't exist, or pretending to be your friend when really they are a big meanie.

Not everyone on the internet is a nice person.

Some might be online to trick innocent people. Or some might not even realise they are being mean but because they are behind a screen, or on the other side of the world, they think their words don't matter much.

You should always question what you see on the internet and talk to your parents, teacher, or an adult you trust to help you navigate what is real and what is not. It will take practice but you will soon know how to be safe – just like you did when you learnt how to ride your bike, or cross a road!

Yes, on occasion you may fall, just as you might have scraped your knee when biking but with the right help, you will learn from these accidents and be smarter for it. It is all about practicing.

It is the same with the internet. Sometimes you might click on something that you shouldn't have clicked on. The best thing is to immediately tell an adult that you trust.

You can always get help if you ask for it from a trusted adult – like a teacher, your parents, or maybe a family friend. If you try to hide a boo-boo you made on the internet, it can start to become a problem. If someone on the internet tells you not to tell an adult about something happening then that's a big reason to tell an adult you trust right away!

Now that you have a better understanding of what the internet is, let's start the adventures and begin to learn about things you might come across while wandering through the shadow world.

Group Questions

Question 1. What's your favourite thing to do on the internet?

Question 2. Have you seen something on the internet you didn't think was real or telling the truth? What was it?

Question 3. If you could talk to anyone in the world through the internet, who would it be and what would you say?

Viruses, Applications, Ads – Ahh!

If you have spent time on the internet, you will know that you can easily spend quite a bit of time in the search for new things, new websites, new games and new adventures. It can be a fun place to explore but we need to know what lies in the shadows around us. If you wander off the beaten path, you might find yourself in a little spot of bother.

What do we mean? Let's jump into an adventure with Tui!

Tui often jumps on her mum's work computer to find a game to play while she waits for her mum to finish work. Tui has a look on the computer and there isn't much to choose from – just solitaire, boring! Tui likes adventure games, so she searches Google by typing 'free adventure games'. She scans the results, finding quite a few to pick from. She finds one of interest; a fairy goblin game and it looks fun. She clicks the link and downloads the game. Once it finishes, she clicks on the file to run the app (game) installer. She then just clicks 'OKAY' on all of the pop-up request boxes, letting the download do what it needs to do to install. Once done, she opens the game and enjoys playing with it for twenty minutes or so before her mum is ready to go home. It was an awesome game!

Little did Tui know that she had downloaded the game from a malicious (bad) site – the game she installed was what is known as a 'trojan horse' and it carries a virus that it has also installed. This virus will spread through her mother's computer and also onto the rest of the machines in her mother's office. Tui had unknowingly entered the shadow world and instead of shining her torch around to check if it was safe to download a game to play, she ended up installing the shadows on her mum's computer and all the computers in the office.

Much like humans, viruses come in many different shapes and sizes with varying results of illness – they can stop your computer from working properly; or they can turn your webcam on; or they can read all your emails and much worse things if they are clever enough. There are many viruses in the shadow world and they all aim to harm your computer and your safety.

Luckily, there are ways to protect ourselves from these shadows. Let's grab our torch and find out how!

First, when you download games, or other applications online, you should always check it's from a legitimate online marketplace that goes with that computer, or phone (like the Apple store iTunes, Windows Marketplace, or the Play store on Android phones). This will massively help you stay out of the shadows as these applications must have the big tick of approval from Apple, Google or Microsoft to be listed. If you download straight from a random unknown website, anyone could have put that game, or application, online and it could contain any type of virus (or be a trick and not even what you think you're downloading!).

Another big issue is that Tui downloaded the game without her mum's permission. Her mum could have helped her visit the Windows

Marketplace to download a fun free game, or her mum may have even offered a different idea for her seeing as it was her work laptop.

Work computers hold a lot of valuable information that the shadows want and it's best to only use them for work and work alone – none of the fun stuff. Keep the fun stuff to your personal home computers and phones.

Viruses can hide in shadows online; they can automatically download when you click on enticing quizzes that might pop up on social media sites like 'what sort of kitten are you', or 'take this quiz to see how much you ACTUALLY love Disney movies'. It's best to avoid clicking on any ads, links, or any pop-ups you see on websites. They can freeze your computer, or they can ask you questions like 'tell me your personal information or I will email all your contacts', or other mean things like that. NEVER believe them. Always remember, if you don't shine your torch on the shadow, it stays scary, so shine your torch on it by telling an adult ASAP!

Computers and phones also hold stuff called anti-virus software that you can buy. A lot of different companies make anti-virus software that checks your computer for any viruses hiding in the shadows before you even get there. Then, it protects you when you accidentally click on something that is a virus. It does this by blocking any downloads but you always need to triple-check that you're clicking on the right thing first.

If you do unintentionally download a virus, it's best to act fast and tell an adult right away. This way, they can call an IT specialist to help them out. Viruses can be stopped. Don't believe what you read if they come up with messages asking for personal information, or other questions to confuse you if they are good or bad. An IT specialist is a phone call away and will help you out of the dark and back to safety! The worst thing to do is to hide it, or to stay quiet about it.

Now we have our virus torch – we know to shine it around a website to make sure it is the right one we want. We know now to only download games, or other applications from the verified places and we know to ask permission before downloading anything.

Group Questions

Question 1. Have you ever downloaded a game or an application through a free random pop up site online? What was it and what made you want to download it? After reading this book, do you think it may have been dodgy?

Question 2. What's your all-time favourite gaming app and how did you find it?

Question 3. Have you ever seen someone download a virus or do you have any stories about people you know who have?

Question 4. What ads do you click the most on? Why do you think you click on them the most?

Gaming and Your Online Friends

Gaming is fun! Online gaming can be awesome also; playing with friends and making new ones is a great way to spend your free time. It can be exciting to explore new worlds on your PlayStation, Xbox, or other online consoles. Let us have an adventure with Richard and see what shadows there can be in the gaming world!

Richard is a good kid; he is ten years old, plays sport on the weekends with mates and loves to play online games when he can. His parents are happy to let him play his games online, trusting he is responsible enough to know right from wrong when dealing with the online world. This is true – Richard does know right from wrong and he plays the games that he told his parents he would. There is something that Richard's parents don't know though – that there are many shadows in these games also!

When Richard plays online games, he plays with many other kids from all round the world, he talks to them on chat platforms about the game and many other things as well. There is a friendly community space and Richard talks to people in it, many of whom he has never actually met. Richard enjoys making new friends with similar interests to him and checking in on his friends he has made there!

In one of his games, he starts to talk to Sara; she has told Richard that she is eleven and from a school just across town from him. They become friends, talking about everything from their families to their schools. Richard forms a crush on Sara, so they exchange phone numbers and even share funny photos with each other.

Richard thinks Sara is a very pretty girl and so they arrange to meet in person one day after school at a sports ground between both their homes. Richard hasn't told his parents about Sara. She is sort of his first crush and he is embarrassed to talk to them about her.

Today is the day he will meet Sara in person! Richard is so excited. School goes quick and after, he rides to the sports ground, where he waits for Sara to arrive. She is late but he doesn't mind; maybe she had to walk or got held up.

The only car he can see is a white van in the parking lot. There is a guy in it and he seems to be watching Richard, which makes him uncomfortable. Maybe he thinks Richard is up to no good and this makes Richard feel self-conscious, or guilty for being here without telling anyone.

The man opens the van door, gets out and walks toward Richard. The man is looking around to see if anyone else is with Richard.

'Hi Richard,' the man says as he comes closer. *How does he know my name?* Richard has a creepy sensation along the hairs on his neck, like there is real trouble coming.

'Who are you?' Richard answers. 'How do you know my name?' he asks the stranger. Richard doesn't know him; he has never seen him before.

'I am here to meet you! My name is Andrew and I love playing games with you; it's a bit silly really but you know me as Sara. We have been talking about meeting for weeks now. It is great to meet you finally! You're such a great friend to have, I just didn't want to freak you out by admitting I wasn't Sara online.'

Richard is very nervous; this isn't right, something is wrong.

'Do you want to come for a drive with me, Richard? We can talk about gaming and things you like to do. I just got a brand-new PlayStation and I was hoping we could play in person?'

Richard knows he should never get in the car with a stranger. He jumps on his bike and dashes away as fast as he can pedal. He is shaken by the whole situation and when he is home, tells his parents about what happened. When he has finished explaining, his parents take him to the local police station so that he can tell them what happened at the park and describe what Andrew looked like to them.

Richard has learnt a very important lesson about the shadows in the gaming world – not everyone is who they say they are. There are good people in the world but we can't trust people online who we haven't met in the real world.

Let's think about this and learn from Richard.

If you have a good friend through the gaming world (or social media), always tell your trusted adult about them because there could be a shadow hiding that they can spot to let you know to shine your torch. Richard was lucky because he was smart enough to escape that situation and did not trust Andrew but people can be convincing at times and you might be too scared to say NO to them. Always remember to be confident and shine your torch. Never meet with people from the online world in real life without an adult knowing or being with you.

Sara from Richard's adventure could have ended up being a real person named Sara – but that wasn't the case. Instead, a strange man got Richard's phone number and tried to convince Richard to go to his house and no adults knew anything about this meeting.

Richard shouldn't feel embarrassed, or ashamed; he should know that in the future all he needs to do is let an adult know, as they might see the shadows that he cannot.

We can learn from Richard and escape situations when they don't feel right and shine our torches around that gaming world to make sure people are who they say they are. Most of all, bring trusted adults along on your adventures – let them know who you're talking to and what you're talking to others about.

Group Questions

Question 1. What is your all-time favourite online game and why? What makes it fun?

Question 2. Have you ever chatted to a person you don't know in real life through a game? Who were they and what cool qualities do they have?

Question 3. Try to name all the ways you could make yourself look like someone else in person (changing your hair, makeup, a silly hat etc), then try to name all the ways you could make yourself look like another person online (a new profile picture maybe?). How hard does changing your appearance in real life versus online seem?

Phishing Emails – Is This Message Too Good to Be True?

Most of you are using emails for schoolwork, or you see your caregivers using emails for work. Emails are a great way to receive messages from other people, learn about shopping specials online, sign up for your favourite brand's discounts and much more!

Are there shadows in emails? You bet there are! Let's have a little adventure with Jenny to check one out and charge up our email shadow torch.

Jenny loves getting emails from her friends at school. She doesn't love all the homework she also gets from school but then, who does? Her dad says that homework teaches you to plan and prioritise work and life. 'A great skill to learn!' he would often declare.

Jenny thinks homework is boring but her dad is very smart, so she works hard to make sure she gets all her homework done before she has any free time for her friends.

Today, while Jenny is checking her emails, something she does after homework, she sees a strange email arrive in her inbox. The email is addressed using Jenny's first and last name and it says that they are very happy they found her. How exciting! Jenny feels special to be noticed and reads the email with honest intent.

The email explains how Jenny's great, great aunt has passed away after being hit by a car. The email further explains that the people writing to her were lawyers and that Jenny was the only person who had been written into her great aunt's will, meaning that all her fortune and land were now Jenny's to own. The fortune was estimated to be thirty million US dollars – wow! The email explains that she had two days to confirm by clicking the link in the email and to provide further details to be identified as the true heir to this vast fortune. Jenny knew her parents were struggling with bills and even fighting a bit because of this.

Jenny would love to share this money and help make their lives better.

Jenny clicks on the link in the email as instructed and fills out the form with all her details. It asks for her bank details to deposit the money, or bank card information to transfer it there, so she takes her mum's card out of her wallet. She wants to keep this amazing fortune a secret until she has the money for them. They will be so happy about this!

She submits the form and then goes back to looking at her other emails. It's a good day. Jenny is one happy and excited wee thing!

About thirty minutes go by and Jenny has finished her homework. She leaves her computer to head downstairs when she hears her mum crying to her dad. 'It is all gone, Tom, all of it! How could all our money just disappear out of our bank account?'

'Someone must have got our card details from somewhere; they've drained all of our money!' her dad replies and Jenny can hear they are very upset.

Jenny starts to feel sick in her belly – she only just shared that information online and now her mum is saying they have no money at all?

Could this have been because of her?

She doesn't want to tell her parents what she has done but she takes a big breath in and decides shadows can only be dealt with when the lights are on. She rushes to her mum, crying and telling her all about the email she received and how Jenny thought she was saving the family from money problems and was just trying to help. Jenny is beside herself with guilt because she fell into an email trap sent by the shadow without even realising it, not until it was too late.

Let's learn with Jenny and see how we can avoid making the same mistake.

Her dad sits her down and he explains to her that she had fallen for a SCAM. The email was not real; she was not going to inherit a fortune. The information she had given them allowed them to find the bank account and when Jenny clicked on the email link, the scammers were able to locate her computer in order to remotely access the account and steal all of their money.

Jenny didn't do this on purpose; Jenny is a good girl but these sorts of emails are very common and we all need to understand that you shouldn't give out information like this to strangers, even if what they are offering is too good to pass on.

Jenny now has her torch on emails and has learnt the lesson that we shouldn't click on emails that come from people we don't know, or if they make offers too good to be true! She knows that if you don't know who it is from then it is an unsafe email and is from the shadow world. We always need to be careful with any emails like this and ask our parents, or another adult we trust for help if we're not sure if they are real, or SCAMS.

What these are called are PHISHING emails – you say it like fishing. Much like fishing, these mean people use 'bait' in these emails that attracts you to the amazing offer. This 'bait' is something to make you excited and encourages you to click on the link or reply to them with what they request. It could be in the form of telling you they want to give you money, or they may pretend to be someone else that you like talking to or want to hear from. There are many types of 'bait' they use but just remember, don't take a bite and don't reply; don't click a link, or do what they tell you to do without triple-checking first!

There are a lot of different things from the shadow world that can come through your emails. It could be addressed to you using your full name, it could use personal details few know, or it could tell you they have 'dirt' on you that they will share if you don't do certain things for them or reply with certain information – NEVER trust these emails!

Use your charged-up email torch to shine a big, bright light on these shadows and if you don't know if an email is real or not, let an adult know and get them to double-check it.

Group Questions

Question 1. What is the best email you have ever received, the one that makes you the happiest when you think about it?

Question 2. Have you ever had any emails like the ones we have mentioned here? Ones that make you go 'hmmm, that seems too good to be true', or make you question if they are telling the truth? What were they?

Question 3. If you received an email saying you HAD to click on a link, or the only way to get what the email promises is to click a link – what would you do first?

Question 4. If you could email anyone in the whole world and they would reply – who would it be?

Password123!

We don't use the same key to get into our houses, our cars, or to access our diaries, or even to open treasure chests – so let's not use the same password for every site we need to visit and log-in for! Most websites you join need you to enter a password, or even your computer when you open it, or your phone when you unlock it.

The best way to remember this password lesson in one sentence is: if you use the same password for everything and the shadow world finds out what that password is, it can now get into all your accounts! Not good.

Let's join Garry to see why that's an important lesson and earn our password torch beam!

Garry is Annie's dad and he is a very busy man.

He is a stay-at-home dad who works part-time doing basic handyman jobs for people around his neighbourhood. Garry isn't the best with computers but he has been improving his skills over time as he uses them to generate invoices for the work he does and to pay the family's bills via internet banking.

Garry uses the same password for ALL his online accounts because it's easier to remember than trying to remember many different passwords. He would even forget his head if it wasn't screwed on sometimes! He uses the same password for internet banking, the online accounting portal, emails for his business and some social media accounts like Facebook, which he uses often to keep in touch with old school friends.

One day, Garry receives an email from a potential customer with a document attached. It says there are some pictures and information about the job they would like Garry to do for them. The email address or name isn't one Garry recognises but that's not unusual with his work. He gets a lot of jobs by word of mouth; this is when people tell other people how good of a job he does.

Garry decides to open the file and, when he does, it comes up with a login screen for him to log in to his emails so he can get the file. That's strange as he is already logged into the emails but he shrugs it off and puts in his details. When he does, the box drops away and the document opens. As he expected.

The document is a strange garble of information that doesn't even make any sense. Oh well, no matter, he moves on and finishes off his invoicing before heading out to his bank to deposit some cash he got for a job yesterday.

Using your knowledge torch that has been charged up through our email and scam chapters, can you guess what happened when Garry opened that file and entered the information to log into his emails?

The pop-up box that he entered his details into was a fake window that was opened by the document he clicked on. The cybercriminal (the person from the shadow world in this story) who had sent Garry the email made the document so that when he opened it, it would execute a program or app to bring that window up and capture Garry's information when he types it in. It also gave them access to Garry's computer so that when he finished up doing his invoices and left the computer on, they could do whatever they wanted.

If you have read this book in order, you will realise that this has downloaded a type of virus on Garry's computer.

If Garry had used different passwords for each of his different accounts, the bad guy in this story would have only been able to get into Garry's email, which is still not a great thing but it would have minimised what they could have done. However, we all know Garry didn't use different passwords in his accounts; they are all the same password.

So, when the shadow person went into the online banking and tried the same password, they were able to log in and transfer out all the money in the accounts. Then they went into Garry's invoicing platform and they changed the details of the bank account that customers should pay their money into when Garry did work for them. So, while Garry is doing lots of great work for his clients, he is going to be wondering why none of them are paying him. This could go on for months before he notices the details have been changed. Poor Garry!

So, when we shine our torch on this shadow

we learn that if Garry had different passwords for all these different things, the shadow person could have only gotten his emails and nothing else.

You don't wear the same underwear four days in a row (gross, I know), so don't do it with your passwords! Use new ones, make them fun and make them long (three or four words) like 'monkey disco mash', or 'snake tree pie'. Make it something you remember but very hard for the shadow guys and girls to guess, learn or try for multiple logins.

So go change your passwords now and make them unique and remember Garry's story as the years go by as it will keep you much safer in the digital world.

Sometimes the shadow world does get in but we have to use our torches as much as possible to know how to equip ourselves to make their impact as little as possible.

Group Questions

Question 1. If you were a super spy and you needed to get into a locked door QUICK, would you prefer to have a big stack of different keys to sift through to find the right one, or a big pile of keys that are all the exact same to choose from?

Question 2. How do you think of the passwords you use?

Question 3. Do you use a password manager? How do you remember your passwords?

Question 4. Have you ever had an online account hacked or have any of your friends or family?

Social Media and Snakes

Social media is fun and you can discover a lot of things that will interest you! It's a great way to keep in touch with friends and family. But unfortunately, social media has a lot of shadows we need to be aware of.

Social media is a place where it's easy to be someone you're not, it's a place where someone can trick other people into thinking they are a different age, or even a whole different person!

People can edit their photos to show themselves as looking perfect, or they edit out things they don't like about the way they look. They can pretend to have a whole different life than what they really have.

This is fine and people can choose what they post online but always remember to never compare yourself to someone you see on social media, as chances are even they don't look like that!

Whenever you look at social media, always remember to keep in the back of your mind that it may not be the whole truth. By remembering that, you can make sure you are keeping safe and not trusting meanies, or not comparing yourself to anyone else.

Now let's join Kirra on an adventure and warm our torches up to shine around the world of social media and uncover what we should be avoiding for this to be less scary so we can focus on the fun!

Kirra is a girl in year six; she has lots of friends and she loves to dance or hang out at the park with them. One day she decided that she was going to sign up for some social media accounts like TikTok, Instagram, Snapchat and Facebook. All of her friends have accounts and she wants to share all of her fun adventures with them!

She downloads the apps on her phone but she doesn't check with her parents if this is okay.

Kirra thinks a few of her friends are doing it so there can't be anything wrong with her doing it too. She opens the apps on her phone, filling in all the information they ask for like when she was born, her phone number, her address, her email address and a few other questions about her. Kirra thinks it must be okay for her to give all this information out. They wouldn't ask her for it if it wasn't needed, right? The app asks her if she would like to make her contact information and her date of birth publicly visible. Kirra considers it for a moment and decides that she should make it visible so that her friends can see it and know how to get in contact with her if they need to.

Kirra gets a bunch of friend requests from all the kids at her school; she is loving it! She starts getting a lot of likes and comments on her photos. Kirra then starts getting friend requests, follows and adds from people she doesn't recognise. She must know them from somewhere because they're adding her, she decides. A lot of them have profile pictures of horses (her favourite animal) and her favourite cartoons, so she trusts them and accepts the requests so she can get more likes and comments.

Kirra goes about her life, not thinking much about the new apps or all the information she has shared. She posts photos and videos with her new friends she has added to the apps. She shares pictures of her at the park, at school and in dance class. She is getting a lot of new friends, boys and girls of all ages. The likes are flooding in!

When you've been on a bushwalk, has anyone ever told you that even if you don't see a snake or spider, they could be seeing you? We're taught to always walk cautiously through bushland to make sure we're not bitten by snakes or spiders because even if we can't see them, chances are they can see us.

Social media can be the same with its many shadows and Kirra is about to find this out.

One day, when Kirra is walking home from school, she feels like someone is watching her.

It's a weird feeling but she looks around and doesn't see anyone. She walks a little faster, as she is only a few blocks from home. Suddenly an older man steps out in front of her.

'You're Kirra, aren't you? I have been watching you on TikTok. We are friends on Facebook as well. I LOVE your photos and videos. You're great! Do you live around here too? I live close by,' the man says.

Kirra feels a bit awkward; he is a bit old to be talking to her. She just mumbles, 'Oh, hi. Yes, that is me. Thank you, I do live around here, yeah.' She steps around him.

He follows her, continuing to talk to her. 'I must admit, I saw your address on your contact information on Facebook and thought since I was so close, I would come and see you!' He laughs and playfully touches her arm.

Kirra thinks fast and, like a smart girl, she pushes his hand off but she is starting to panic. She doesn't think he is a nice guy – she needs to get home and fast.

Kirra says she forgot something at home and turns to run back to her house. She goes straight to her mum and tells her what just happened. Her mum calms her and they immediately sit down to alter some of those settings on Kirra's social media accounts. Kirra's mum also calls her local police station to let them know what just happened to make sure Kirra was safe. Kirra never sees the man again but this situation could have been much scarier.

We know this is a scary story about Kirra and a terrible shadow world she ended up in but it is one of the lessons we must learn together, to help keep us safe!

If we know what is right and what is wrong, we know how to make sure we stay safe.

Let's break down what we should be looking for with our torches to make sure we are keeping ourselves safe on social media.

The first thing we can learn from this is that Kirra's account was public and that she was also accepting friend requests from people she didn't know. The apps had asked for her personal information like date of birth, address and contact numbers and she put them all in and made that information public also.

Always remember to put in the bare minimum when signing up online. Often, they don't need you to put in those details, so just leave it blank. Remember when the website asked Kirra if she wanted to keep her information private or make it public and she clicked public, which means anyone could see it? Private is always the way to go.

This means people have less chance of finding these things out about you, things that aren't any of their business anyway. People can be nosy, especially online, so the best thing to do is click on private every time. The people that love and care about you will know these details, anyway.

Kirra installed the social media account

apps and signed up without first talking to her parents or trusted adults around her. Making your first social media accounts can be a big deal, the information or photos and videos you post can be in cyberspace forever. But it is also exciting and fun! Involve your trusted adults in this process so you can talk about why you want social media and set some boundaries that will help keep you safe. It's like training wheels for your bike: until you know how to ride by yourself, it's best to rely on your trusted adults for safety. The same goes for social media!

If your trusted adults say you are not quite ready for social media, you should listen to them and their reasons. I know it may be upsetting because you want to be like your friends but they will only be doing it to keep you safe and that is the most important thing! Remember, adults have used social media for a long time now and they know what shadows to look out for. They may not be able to explain it in ways you can understand immediately but if they say no, they will have a very good reason for it.

Kirra did the right thing by going straight to her mum after the run-in with the man; it is important to let an adult know if something like that ever occurs. I am sure your trusted adults have already talked to you all about chatting with strangers and this falls into that same basket. On the internet, it's a wee bit easier for strangers, as people can hide behind a screen and pretend to be people they're not.

So now, when we use social media (if that's now or in the future), remember to use your knowledge torch and make sure you're not making your profile public. Make sure you're not letting strangers spy and be nosy looking at what you're posting. Make sure to double-check that the person who is adding you as a friend is your friend.

Most of all, involve your trusted adults in the process of your social media account setup and how you use it. If something isn't right, tell them straight away. Your trusted adult could be a teacher, someone from the police, your parents, guardians, or a family friend. They care about you and they will likely know how to keep you safe from any shadows.

Group Questions

Question 1. Do you use social media? What accounts do you have?

Question 2. What is your favourite social media account to use and why? What makes it fun?

Question 3. What sort of things do you share on your social media account or accounts? Or, if you don't have one yet – what sort of things will you share? What are your favourite things to show the world?

Question 4. Would you let strangers come up to you on the street and start "following" you? Or people with cartoon pictures as faces talk to you on the street? Maybe not! Would you let strangers do this online now after reading this? If no – why? If yes – why?

Your Unique Superpower and the Villains Who Bully It

This is a very important chapter, maybe one of the most important in this book. This could be a little confronting for you but it's a topic that we need to discuss.

Bullies are a problem that have been around for as long as humans have been on Earth. There are endless reasons why people are bullies, sometimes it's accidental but often it's on purpose. A lot of bullies are insecure and they lash out at others to try and make themselves feel better – everyone has their own story to make them act the way they do.

Most of you will have been bullied at some point in your lives and I'm sure you'll agree that it is not a great experience. You may have even bullied someone at some point in your lives, sometimes without even knowing you are doing it. It could be a comment you made online or in person that hurt the other person's feelings, or if you are a bully that does it on purpose, you really need to pay attention to this chapter because it's not a good way to use the precious life you have been gifted and when you grow up you'll be ashamed that you acted that way. Bullying can be very upsetting and challenging – it can cause ripple effects in people's lives that do a lot of long-lasting damage. No one likes to be picked on and teased by someone for being different when they're just being themselves.

We are all different and we should embrace that. Our differences are our superpowers!

Someone's superpower is no reason for anyone to be singled out, to be teased or made miserable, or to be used to help bullies show off in front of others or to make themselves feel better. This exact same message we learn in our physical lives applies to our lives online too. It's much easier to write hurtful things online than it is to say it to someone's face which is why cyber-bullying is such a frequent occurrence.

Do you know what you should do if you meet

someone who is different to you? Someone with a different culture or someone who has grown up speaking a different language than you? You should learn from them and in turn, they can learn from you. You could hear interesting new stories from them or ways to do things, or even learn how to speak a new language from them!

If we embrace 'different', it will make all our lives better! We will learn more and be happier for it.

In this chapter, we're not going to join anyone's story but instead, have a little think about your own story. Think about times when you have been bullied or made to feel bad by other people and instead of letting that feeling turn to anger, think about how you can stop that feeling from happening for others. We like to think about why that person said mean things to us – could someone have been mean to them that day and they were sad about it and lashed out? Could we intimidate them? Could they be jealous of us? There are so many reasons why people can be hurtful to others but always remember to take a higher road and not pass on that hurtfulness or hate to other people, whether it's in person or online.

This time, let's charge up our torches with some emotional knowledge about how to be better people and not let our emotions run wild. This will help keep our emotions from spilling out into the virtual world where it's easy to say mean or hurtful things to a stranger online.

What should you do if you are bullied in person in the real world or online in the digital world? You should tell your trusted adults and teachers. I know, it's embarrassing and no one wants to talk about this but you shouldn't keep this to yourself – you should be able to talk to adults about it.

Bullies can say some awful things online because they think they can stay anonymous or that everyone will believe them if they say they have pictures or videos of you that they will share to the world if you tell on them, or don't do what they tell you to do. It's important to remember that most of the time they are lying.

If they're not lying, then to leak pictures or videos of someone who doesn't want them shown is illegal and the police will help you out.

If you are bullied online, do not believe the bully. Do not give them time out of your glorious day. Delete and block them off whatever platform they are using to contact you. You know when you go fishing, you use bait on your hook to catch a fish? Cyberbullies often use empty threats of having embarrassing information or footage of you as bait so you bite their hook and they can reel you in. Stay swimming around the ocean like the strong shark you are and don't fall for the cyberbullies' bait.

What these cyberbullies don't know is that everything online is tracked. Your IP address is your computer's own little signature, which can be tracked. Any time someone posts something online it can be tracked back to who posted it – even if they think they're anonymous. Your local police and even the federal police have whole teams dedicated to this – they can track down cyberbullies who are saying awful things or who try to get you to do weird things. You just need to tell a trusted adult or even a police officer so they can help you.

We are stronger together and if we stand tall as one and say it is not okay to be mean to others just because someone has had a bad day, or they are jealous or different to you, together we can stop this. Let's not accept bullies in person or online and make them understand that bullying behaviour is not accepted. If bullies can understand their mistakes, they can change their behaviour.

If you learn just one thing from this chapter, it should be this: different is good, not something that anyone should be embarrassed about.

Be yourself and love who you are – you may not know it now but whatever makes you different could be your superpower when you grow up.

Group Questions

Question 1. Have you ever done something online that you regret? Have you ever said something to, or about another person that you probably shouldn't have? What was it and how did it make you feel during and afterwards?

_____

_____

_____

_____

Question 2. Have you ever experienced a form of bullying online? What happened?

_____

_____

_____

_____

_____

Question 3. What do you think the best thing to do is when you find yourself getting angry at someone online?

Question 4. What do you think the best thing to do is when you find someone is being mean to you online?

Ahhh-Choo! I've Caught the Flu!

Don't be silly, you can't catch the flu online!

But wait... actually, you can in a way! You can get what people call a computer virus. A computer virus infects your computer or mobile devices (like tablets and phones) just like the flu would in a person.

Much like awful colds, computer viruses can cause major disruption and sometimes catastrophic results.

Like humans with a virus, a computer virus can change in how serious it is.

Some of them can just be annoying with pop-ups on your screen, they can slow your machine down or they could cause your device to completely shut down and not work at all. In some situations, they can even cause you to lose all your saved files like photos, emails or even homework! Try explaining that to your teacher – 'Sorry, Miss, my computer caught a cold' might not be the best way to say it!

Now, as you have just found out, letting your computer get a cold is not such a good idea but what can you do to help avoid getting one? That's simple actually! We don't even need to jump into a story with any of our new friends we're meeting throughout this book, let's just charge up our torch by listing out a few things you can do.

One – You need to make sure that your device has anti-virus protection. This is like getting a vaccination for your computer. We've talked about it in a couple of our stories so far; it will help keep you and your device safe while on the internet and when opening files or clicking links. If your computer doesn't have one of these, you should talk to your trusted adults about this. It's a small cost and can save you and your family lots of money for repairs or recovery efforts when or if something does happen.

Two – Don't download apps or files from places you don't know are trustworthy. If it's a device like an iPad or Android, get the apps or games from those providers' (Apple, Google Play or Microsoft) online app stores. It will help keep you and your device flu-free, or at least help reduce your risk.

Three – Make sure all your devices are updated to the latest version of the software available. If you are unsure, ask your teacher, your parents, or your trusted adults to help you do this.

Four – This is a very important one. Don't go to dodgy-looking websites that you shouldn't be on! If you use common sense and do the right things while you are online, you won't need to worry about having to take your computer to the hospital (your local computer repair shop) because they will stay clean and happy.

Sometimes cool or weird-looking websites might pop up, ones that are luring you over with cool-looking toys, games, R18 adult stuff or weird things that might look interesting to check out and you may accidentally click on one. As soon as you click on one of these websites, it might download a virus silently without you even knowing. It's an easy mistake to make but just let a trusted adult know as soon as possible, informing them that it was an honest mistake. Then they can fix it at the computer repair shop, instead of some bad virus lurking in the background.

Communication and honesty are always the best policy, we know it's easy to fall down a hole when you don't have your torch on in the dark!

Group Questions

Question 1. Do you have an anti-virus on your home computer or mobile device?

Question 2. Has your home computer ever been backed up? Why do you think this is important to do?

Question 3. What do you think is the best thing to do if you accidentally download a computer virus?

Metadata? Meta Whaaaat?

Everyone loves to share their adventures with their friends and family, right? We know we love telling people about cool things that just happened, or showing them some photos of birthday parties or awesome things we've seen. It is great to be proud of the things you do and to share the fun times with others!

But before we share these things like photos, videos or even just comments about where we are on any social media sites (like Facebook, Instagram, TikTok – the list goes on!), we should think about what we are posting and why.

Let's charge up our privacy torches with a little story with Leah.

Leah has just turned thirteen years old – woohoo! She had a super fun day horse riding, then a sleepover with all her friends, complete with a movie night. Leah and her friends were sharing photos all day and night, riding ponies, having dinner and watching movies. The night was fun and they wanted to share it!

A couple of hours later, Leah and her friends started getting weird message requests on their social media profiles from people that they didn't know. The messages were saying things like, 'We know what house you're in and we know you're together and having a party, can we come over?' One of them even tried to force Leah into sending more photos, saying, 'Please send more photos of your birthday party. I love seeing you girls having fun.' It was really odd!

Leah called down to her foster mum Joyce who came up to see what the fuss was about. Leah showed Joyce the messages and luckily Joyce knew exactly what to do. She asked the girls to all sit with her as she explained a little bit about what had happened and how to stop it.

The first thing Joyce did was make sure the girls' social media profiles were set to private (which we learnt a few chapters ago). Joyce then 'blocked' all these weird messages from the girls' social media accounts and clicked on settings to turn on 'do not allow new message requests'. This means these oddballs couldn't get through or see their photos anymore.

Once the immediate changes had been made, Joyce then explained how and why these messages were coming through. She said in these photos, a bad person like a bully, or even a stranger with weird intentions that found one of Leah's social media profiles, could look at these photos and might be able to see Leah's and her friends' location. Most photos have what is called metadata inside them. You can't see it but it provides people (or special software programs) more information about things like the date it was taken, the time and even exact GPS locations of where the photo was taken. If you have tracking turned on in your phone, or computer and it has a Wi-Fi connection to allow you to post on the internet, it can automatically put this information in the photo.

Joyce told the girls that someone who may want to know more about where they are could take that GPS information from the metadata in the photo and it would give them your exact location! Creepy, huh? They could come to your home, the school, the playground or watch your sports game – wherever you are. There are lots of different reasons why bad people may want to do this but none of them are okay – it is an invasion of your privacy. Sometimes people track down GPS locations because they worry about a person's safety but most times it's for reasons that are a bit scarier, which is why we must be careful with what we post online and how much information we let strangers access. We all want to stay safe!

Let's learn from Leah (and her expert foster mum Joyce) and firstly, turn off location services on your phones, tablets and computers and only turn them on when you need them (like if you're using a maps app to find something, for example). If you don't know how to, ask your trusted adults or teacher and they will be able to help you do this. If they don't know how to, ask them to Google it and it's as simple as pie!

Photos can also reveal information about your date of birth, who you are friends with and where you normally hang out. All this stuff can be used to track you down and, as we mentioned above, it's not always for nice reasons. There are many reasons why we are taught not to talk to strangers, this falls under that situation. Some strangers may be nice but a lot are not. As a rule, it's best to stay safe and stay private.

Another handy hint with photos: if you want to make sure no exact GPS metadata is captured in your photo, you can always screenshot your original photo and post that screenshot instead. It won't be as good a resolution but better safe than sorry until you have your knowledge torch fully charged up and ready to know exactly who is seeing your posts and how to get rid of the weird message requests from strangers!

Group Questions

Question 1. What are your favourite photos and videos to share online? What is your favourite social media platform to share them on or send them through?

_____
_____
_____
_____
_____

Question 2. If you do share pictures and videos, have a look at the last five that you posted and try to spot unique identifying things in them, things like the background showing street signs, or important information. Get your detective on! After you've spotted all those things, think about how easy it would be for someone to find out where those photos were taken.

Question 3. Do you think it's a good idea to post online about your birthday party, your friends' or your family's birthday parties? What information could you be giving out by doing this? What do you think people should double check before they upload photos of a party?

I Have Your Videos, Don't Make Me Share Them ...

Many of you that already use the internet or have phones and computers would have your trusted adults asking you what you do online. They might be asking what you see, who you talk to and what apps you install. If they don't ask you things like that, it must mean they really trust you, which is awesome but it's best to still chat to them about what you're up to and what you're doing – so if you're ever in a pickle, they can help.

If you have read this book from front to back, you will probably see a theme happening but if this is the first chapter you have jumped to then you need to understand that the internet and the online world are not safe. We need to be a step ahead of the bad people by having fully charged knowledge torches so we can avoid the scary shadows – shining a light on them and taking problems away (or lessening them).

You may feel that your trusted adults are nagging you when they ask what you are doing online or when they lock your devices down to help prevent you from going to particular websites or installing games and other applications. It is out of love; they just want to protect you from the dangers in the online world as they do in the real world.

Adults may not know everything (like sometimes they think they do) but most of them have been using the internet and have been online for most of their lives so chances are they will have experienced everything you may experience. Some of it may be embarrassing, some of it may be scary, some of it may just be silly. You may even have trusted adults that don't use the internet but the main point here is that you are never alone in what you experience online.

The world can be a dangerous and scary place at times. The same can be said about the online world (the shadow world of the internet), which we are merging more and more with our real lives. It's part of our lives in almost every aspect and as our virtual and physical lives continue to merge, you will all need to learn to identify and avoid these shadows for yourselves, maybe even help your trusted adults and friends see them. They are still learning just like you and me.

Let's jump into a quick story with Kat – it's a weird one but unfortunately a common one!

Kat uses her laptop every day for schoolwork; she leaves it open in her room all day and uses it in the evenings before dinner. One day, she gets an email from a weird address she hasn't seen before. The email says, 'We have been watching you through your webcam and will send a video to your entire school email contact list and social media sites of you changing into your PJs, if you don't do what we say.' Gross, right? People online can be weird sometimes.

Kat immediately is terrified and believes the email; she panics and even vomits as she imagines her teachers and friends opening an email with a video of her in it! She replies to the email by saying, 'No, please don't share it. I'll do whatever you want just don't share it.'

She gets an email back where the bad people

are asking her to do really confusing things like sending more videos and photos of herself.

Kat doesn't know what to do. She sits on her bed and cries, at a loss of what to do until her uncle Adrian, concerned for her crying, knocks on the door and she lets him in; immediately collapsing into his arms, sobbing with tears. She just points to the laptop and he checks it out. She wouldn't have felt comfortable showing her stepmum or her dad these emails but Uncle Adrian is one of her pals. She trusts him.

Telling Adrian was the best thing Kat could have done and she should be super proud of herself for doing it. Adrian knows that these emails are not okay and are illegal. If you have read the other chapters, you'll know that this sort of pressuring, or bullying, of people is taken very seriously by the police and it is never, ever your fault. Even if you have taken the photos, or videos these bullies are trying to blackmail (force you to do something or they will leak it) you with, it is still illegal for them to have forced access and it's very illegal for them to try and make you send them more.

Adrian immediately calls his local police and

they arrive within the hour. They assure Kat everything is okay and they check her computer to see what exactly happened. They get their cyber experts on the case and it turns out that the people in the email were actually lying the whole time – they never had a video of Kat, they were just trying to get her to send them some, using the lie of having a video as bait to make her do it.

So, from Kat's scary story, what have we learnt?

First, we know that a bad person trying to make you do something online is never okay and you should never do what they ask you to do. Most of the time, these bad people try to say they have this information – photos or videos of you – but they don't. They're lying to try and get what they want and we all know liars are not good.

It's such a stressful situation to be in when you are being bullied or pressured into things – it should never happen but unfortunately in life, it often does. The part about Kat's story that she should be the proudest of is telling her uncle Adrian. She used her smarts to choose the right trusted adult to help her out of this situation. Remember our chapter on bullying? Together we are stronger. This situation is the perfect example of that being the case.

Kat was lucky because the bad people were just lying but a lot of the time if you do get a virus that we learnt about earlier, bad people can record you through your webcam. That's why it's always best to get a webcam cover for your computers and make sure you know where your photos are stored (for example, if they are uploaded to your cloud account or not). Even if these bad people did have a recording of Kat, she handled the situation correctly by involving her trusted adult Adrian and in turn, Adrian handled it perfectly by calling the police.

If you don't have a trusted adult that you feel comfortable with should this ever happen to you, you can just call your local police or go to the station. You will never, ever get the blame or get told off for this – it is not your fault and it never will be.

So, after learning a little bit about what can happen in a bad scenario with Kat, how about you use your charged-up personal safety torch and do something for your trusted adults and your friends? Next time your trusted adults ask you what you have been doing online, what apps you have downloaded or what websites you have visited, don't get angry or frustrated with them. Instead, think about why they are asking this. It is for you and your safety. Remember, they love you and there is a strong chance something bad may have happened to them online when they were younger, so they are worried it'll happen to you also.

Everyone can be shy about different things; maybe your trusted adults are shy about talking about this sort of stuff with you because they want to protect you from the shadow world of the internet. They may not want you to know that these bad people are online yet because they want you to stay happy and carefree but unfortunately, it is for your own good. Have your knowledge torch as bright as possible so you can uncover these mean people, never believe them and be strong and confident to stay bright and happy even when these awful things may happen.

Help your trusted adults and friends to help you by telling them what you are doing online.

Be honest, don't hide things from them – even if you mess up and do something you shouldn't. Everyone messes up in life but the important thing is owning up to your mistakes and learning from them!

You will most likely find the more open you are with your trusted adults, the more freedom they will give you online because they will be able to trust that if you need them you will ask. You can tell them your knowledge torch is fully charged to check for online shadows and that you will talk to them straight away if something seems strange, off, or weird.

The goal of this chapter's conclusion boils down to one main topic from us: to try and make a point in your life where you strengthen your online confidence, where you realise most trusted adults have lived what you are living through, that they know everyone messes up sometimes but they are here for you if you ever do. Practice strengthening your confidence to talk about what you're doing online, about what emails you receive and try to think of a trusted adult you could go to if things do go badly – can you think of one now?

Maybe it's your mum or dad, stepmum or stepdad, foster parent, aunty or uncle, a local police officer, maybe it's one of your parents' friends or even one of your friends' parents or a teacher or sports coach. Try to think of at least one so you are prepared – even have a chat with them about this chapter and use our book as a reason to start a conversation.

It can be as easy as, 'Hey (trusted adult), today I read this super cool, super awesome cyber security book that teaches us about some of the shadows of the cyber world and how to spot what lies within them so we can be safe. It had a scary chapter about a girl named Kat who received an email from bad people saying they had videos of her getting changed and that they would leak them if she didn't do what they say. In the book, Kat told her trusted adult, who was her uncle, who called the police and fixed everything. If something like that ever happened to me, can I come to you?'

Let's hope nothing bad ever happens to you online but if it does, life is a lot less stressful and easier to deal with things when you know you have someone on your side! If you don't feel comfortable chatting to an adult about this yet, maybe start a chat with your school teacher, counsellor, or even just a friend so you can start building that confidence up. After all, in life, confidence is key!

Be open, be honest and do what will keep you and everyone around you safe.

Lies or dishonesty (that includes not telling the whole truth!) always go wrong, so it's best to be open and honest from the start.

You got this, our little shadow slayers!

Group Questions

Question 1. Do you have a webcam on your laptop? If you do, have you ever thought about getting a webcam cover? Why do you think a webcam cover could be handy?

Question 2. This is a question for you to just answer in your head. No need to say it aloud and if you're a trusted adult reading this with your cyber superhero – please keep this answer for them and them alone.

If you found yourself in a situation where someone was pressuring you into doing something online, who would be the first adult you told? Who would be the second? Who would be the third? It's important to know who to reach out to before something like this may happen. Even have a chat with them before something bad happens, telling them that they are your 'emergency' go to. Now, with the trusted adult you are with (or alone) – what would you say to an adult if you had been threatened or blackmailed online? How would you tell them and start the conversation?

Question 3. What is the number of your local police station that you could call if someone was trying to pressure you into sharing something online or if they were threatening you with blackmail? This will be the local (not emergency number as you likely know that one!) number of your police station. Search this number online and write it down to keep it safe, hopefully you'll never need it, but it's better just in case. If you were a police officer, what would you say if someone called you and they were being blackmailed online? What would you say to them to reassure them that it is not their fault and they are not the ones to blame?

The Invasion of the Super Spies – the Internet of Things

What on Earth is the 'Internet of Things (IoT)'? It seems like a silly little made-up saying, doesn't it? Well, it's very real, very cool and quite shadowy!

Let's put IoT into a way that you may be able to easily understand – then it means you can talk about the 'Internet of Things' and you will sound super smart too! Have you ever heard of Alexa, Siri or 'Hey Google'? It's kind of like in superhero movies when a superhero controls his whole house by speaking to it, right? Those operating systems, or 'brains', control the 'IoT' devices – turning them off and on, up and down, around and around – whatever it may be! It's like having a little robot assistant that does stuff for you.

Do you have one of those lights at home that can be turned on from someone's phone? Or smart speakers or cameras in your home? Or have you seen any? Do you have any electronic locks at school or the library that you can open with a pin number? Do you have that fancy air conditioning that you can turn on when you aren't home to make sure it is nice and cool or warm depending on what time of year it is?

These devices are what you would call IoT devices or the full name 'Internet of Things', which just means any device like speakers, lights, doors, cameras or anything that is connected to the internet to make our lives easier. This can be to turn lights on easily or to make them a different colour or to play music while controlling it with a phone. Some crazy cool fridges are even 'smart fridges' that are classed as being part of the 'Internet of Things' because they are connected to the internet and can do things like re-order groceries if it can see you are running out! The world of IoT can be awesome!

These IoT devices are becoming part of our daily lives. They are being put in our roads (like cameras or sensors), they are put in bikes (like GPS tags), skateboards and even clothes. Anything they can think of with any reason to do it, someone somewhere is making them an IoT device. These devices can make life easier but we need to understand some of the shadows, so we know how to shine our lights on them. These devices can listen to us all the time; they can track us wherever we go.

It's important we learn that, just like the internet itself can pose some risks, so too can IoT devices and we should all consider this before we install any strange apps on a smart device. It could allow a bad person to listen in on your family's and friends' conversations. A lot of these conversations might be boring, but these bad people can learn when you are home and when you are not, which means they could break into your home and steal your favourite toy, book – or hey, even TV! We can't have that happening now, can we?

There are many possibilities. Bad people might even decide to lock you and your family outside if you have smart locks on your doors, they might turn the air conditioner on full blast and make it feel like you're in the middle of Antarctica in winter! That wouldn't be so much fun.

So, why don't you ask your trusted adults if they have updated these IoT devices and if they have security features turned on? It might save you an uncomfortable roasting one day or even protect your home from being robbed! It's a simple question that might make a big difference. Your trusted adults will be impressed that you know what the Internet of Things is – they might not even know it's called that themselves, then you get a chance to play teacher!

Have a chat with them or with your friends – the IoT world is very cool when you uncover those shadows and learn how to use them correctly. When you get older and get a house of your own, if you wanted to, you could set up your own superhero house that you could speak to where it could turn on the lights, start robot vacuum cleaners, or even re-stock your fridge – mega cool!

Now if only they made an IoT device to clean your room or do your homework, huh?

Maybe that can be your invention?

Group Questions

Question 1. If you have smart devices in your home or if you've seen them in shops or online – what one is your favourite and why?

Question 2. Do you get ads on your phones or devices after you have spoken out loud about needing to get something? What sort of ads have you got?

Question 3. So we know smart devices record and listen to what you say even when you are not talking to them. What is the funniest thing you can think of that you have said in the last day that a smart device could have heard?

Lock the Door Before You Leave the House! Protect Your Valuables – Your Data

It is becoming more and more normal for people of all ages to have mobile devices for school and social activities. In a lot of schools, you will need a laptop or a tablet/MacBook/iPad or similar device to do your normal school stuff like homework, emails, research and logging into things like online student portals to receive information from your school.

Electronic devices and creating data (like photos, documents, emails – anything really) is probably part of your everyday lives or it will be at some point soon. At your age, you are what is called 'digital natives' – this sort of digital life is probably normal for you and comes as second nature. This might not be the case for many of your trusted adults/parents or even more so, your older trusted adults/grandparents. Computers and portable devices like smartphones were not even thought of when they were kids! You have come to live in a truly exciting time and you will likely see amazing advancements in how the digital world interacts with our real world. The line between the digital world and the real world in the years to come may start to blur.

But let us think about data for a second and how much we all create – data is everywhere! Every time we do anything online or on our devices we leave our digital fingerprint, meaning we made it and it's stored somewhere. What does this mean? Why could this have shadows in it? Let's dive into a story with Jacob.

Jacob is going to high school next year. He has a tablet and a smartphone that he does most of his schoolwork on like getting emails, writing assignments and doing research for school stuff. On those devices, he also plays some games and takes photos and videos of his life, himself and his friends – some for his memories and some for social media platforms.

He has location services on, so all his location

information is stored for apps, photos and the tablet and phone in general. He has a security pin code on both of his devices but it's basic – it's just '1234'. He doesn't want to have to remember something hard and what would anyone do with that stuff anyway?

Let's pause on this story with Jacob and have a think. What do you think would happen if he lost either his tablet or his phone?

If someone found his device or if someone stole it, they could find out where Jacob lives easily because he saved that information in it. They could find out where he goes to school and they could likely login to any of his online accounts as it is almost certain with Jacob's lack of security with his simple pin code, that he would save all his passwords in the device. They could have access to all his data. Silly Jacob, huh? He must not have read our chapter about passwords!

Say someone now has one of Jacob's devices, they guessed his 1234 passcode (after first trying 0000 and 1111, it was the logical next step) and they have been able to wreak havoc with all his data.

They may have been spreading viruses to his

contacts by sending his friends on social media links to click, which they may have opened thinking it was a funny video from Jacob. Now his friends' devices are infected and their data can also be stolen to later cause more trouble.

Because Jacob used both the smartphone and the tablet for the same stuff, he had them linked so all the same data was on both. All his assignments, homework, photos – you name it! This bad person now has access to all Jacob's data and they can delete the lot of it or try to make Jacob pay money to them to get it returned to him. They might even get him to pay and not give him back his data! People can be mean sometimes, which is why we need our knowledge torches so bright.

Jacob could have done some simple things here to protect his data and prevent all his hard work from being stolen, lost or held ransom. If you have read the other chapters, I bet you could name some things he could have done! Try it now before reading what we suggest.

Tried it yet? Okay, let's see how well we match up! We think Jacob could have made his pin code a lot harder to guess. Even better is that most smartphones have a fingerprint login which means only Jacob could access that device. Never use numbers that are that easy to guess or even things like birthdays as they are an easy guess also!

Jacob could have made sure his phone and tablet had different data storage locations and he could have backed up some of his data. This means saving it in different locations as well, so he doesn't lose everything if he loses his device.

A big one that we hope you guessed is passwords again! If Jacob had different passwords to all his accounts, the bad person could only get so far with his device. It would ask them to login to the school portal and the bad person wouldn't know the password or to the social media sites meaning his friends didn't get sent dodgy links to click.

You can see how important it is to think about what is on your devices and, let's be honest, they're easy to lose! They're small and when you have more important things to do like run around with your friends or rush to a sports game, it can be easy to leave a little tablet or phone behind.

Jacob should also think about turning off

the location services on his devices as well just to make sure he's not sharing any information about where he lives, or where he goes – a lot like some of our previous stories. You can turn it back on for apps as needed, it's much safer.

Luckily for Jacob, he's just a silly goose who left his phone (and tablet) on the school bus and someone handed it to the driver after he ran off to play footy with his friends. He would forget his head if it wasn't screwed on!

But, if you're anything like Jacob, when you get to your phone, tablet, laptop or any device of yours next, make that pin code or password stronger and harder to guess. Turn off auto-save passwords and just imagine this...

If a robber was standing in front of two houses and one had a security camera out the front, a padlock on the gate, plus a metal door and the other had a wooden gate with an open latch – which house would they try to rob first? You got it, the easier one. The exact same rule applies to your devices. For a lot of these bad people, this is a numbers game. If something is too hard, like a strong password or pin-code, or multiple security layers, they will give up and move to the next unsuspecting victim.

Protect your data and install your cyber metal gates by getting those pin codes and passwords the strongest they can possibly be!

Group Questions

Question 1. If you had to quickly run out of the house, what three things would you take?
Is your mobile phone, tablet or laptop in those top three?

Question 2. Have you ever lost your device and used the "find my iPhone" or similar apps to find it? How do you think it knows where the phone is?

Question 3. Although we don't think our cyber super heroes ever would be, if you were a hacker – would you try to hack a phone with no anti-virus on it or one with a simple anti-virus software? What would be quicker? What does your answer tell you about why you should have anti-virus on your phone?

Question 4. Can you remotely wipe your device if you lose it? Why do you think this would be good to do?

The Deep Dark Web – the Shadow World's Shadow!

The dark web. It's something you may have heard of – it is like the boogieman that is whispered about, no one knowing what it is, what's on it or where it really is.

We know that the unknown is often interesting, or you may be curious, so we are here now to tell you a little bit about it – because it's better to know why you should be avoiding it, rather than just avoiding it.

The dark web cannot be lit up by our knowledge torches and probably never will be able to – but we can see the outline of the door to it with our torches, so we know where to stay well away from.

In a nutshell, the dark web is a part of the internet that is not shown by search engines;

the websites don't publicly list their location and address information that normal websites would make available so that people can find them. Most people who have websites on the dark web don't want normal people to find their websites, they want them to stay a secret – only allowing certain people to know how to find them.

There are a lot of reasons for this. It's not likely you will ever see the dark web as it is well hidden and is a yucky place to be, so you don't want to search it out. Instead of jumping into a story with someone, we'll give you a little overview of the dark web so your torch knows to illuminate as bright as the sun so you can stay away from it!

Some of the main reasons people have websites, or talk to each other through the dark web are:

- They are doing things that are illegal and don't want to be caught by the police. They want to stay secret.
- They are an unhappy person who wants to meet or talk with other unhappy people and do mean things to unsuspecting people. It's where shadows can meet shadows to create

even more shadows.
- They are a super technical person, a hacker or something like that, who may want a secret and unwatched place to talk with other hackers or very technical people.
- They might want to find out specific information about big companies or share (buy and sell) company data and secrets (like KFC's secret herbs and spices or the CEO's home address) – all illegal stuff and very bad.

There are a lot more reasons than this for someone to be on the dark web but this tells you something very quickly – not much good is happening in these places. For your safety, your friends' safety and your family's safety, you should stay far away from this place. You might wander somewhere that could put you in real physical danger or get you into trouble with the police.

It is like walking down the darkest alley at night in the scariest, spookiest neighbourhood you can imagine with no torch. Not the best thing to do, right?

The dark web isn't a joke and it's no place to try to reach. If you do try to seek out the dark web for a laugh with your friends, nothing good will come of it. People on the dark web are very technical people who can find out all sorts of things about you very easily if you were to try and enter their shadowy world.

Stay on the normal, everyday internet. As we know from other chapters, there are still shadows to look out for – but if you do run into a shadow there, the repercussions are much less and the way to solve it is far easier.

Stay smart, cyber heroes and stay away from the shadows that cannot be lit up!

Group Questions

Question 1. Have you ever heard of the dark web before this? If yes, how? What are some stories you have heard of before?

Question 2. Is the dark web a safe place to look around do you think? Are people nice and safe to be around?

Question 3. If you were a parent and you found out your child was trying to go on the dark web – what would you tell them? What advice would you give them?

Links, URLs, Websites – What?

Links, what are they? Let's first outline what a link is. It is when you get an email from someone and they put in a website they think you should go to for whatever reason. In an email, they would normally have a slight blue tinge to them and when you hover over the top of them, a website address will show up looking something like this:

https://theshadowworld.com.au/

This link is a URL which means it is a website link. If you were to click on this, it would open a web browser like Chrome, Firefox, Safari or Edge, just to name a few options. It would then open the website or whatever is at that location. In a link, you can have it select a file or 'executable file' that would execute (open and start downloading to your device) when clicked.

This is a common option for a bad guy or girl who wants to install one of those viruses we talked about in previous chapters. It could give your PC or device the flu and cause you all sorts of headaches, all from simply clicking on a link! These little executable files can do their thing in sneaky ways too – completely silent in the background so you don't even know they are there or that they have been downloaded.

These links can come to you from many locations. You could get them in emails, Word or PDF documents, text messages or even on websites themselves. You need to be careful when clicking on links and pop-up pictures, especially when they are from someone you don't know, or a website you don't know or wouldn't normally use.

Nick is going to teach us a bit more about links in his story. Thanks, Nick!

Nick was out doing his after-school job – a newspaper delivery job around his neighbourhood (and yes, before you ask, people still have physical papers delivered!). Nick was about halfway through his job when he received a text message from a number he didn't know. It said he had won a $500 voucher for the local cinema. Nick loves a good romance movie, especially on the big screen. He was very excited about his win! What a day today is!

The text said that Nick needed to click on the link and fill out the form with his details to claim the prize. Simple!

Nick immediately clicked on the link and his phone screen flickered for a second. That's weird... He clicked his phone screen on and off again and then it worked fine so he filled out his name, address, email, date of birth and phone number then hit submit. Woohoo! He put his phone back in his pocket and kept on going with his route. He was pumped about the voucher; maybe he could go to the cinema tonight, maybe he could get the confidence to ask Becky from class to even go with him – he had a little crush on Becky.

He continued his job for the next couple of hours and then headed home. When he made it home, he opened his internet banking app on his phone – he had his own account that his pay of $50 a week for the paper route gets deposited into each week. Nick has big plans in life and wants to start his own business one day, so he's started saving already. He's eager to see if he's been paid for the week.

He has a balance of a little over $1000! He has been saving for a long time. Whether he gets the voucher today or not, he decides he has the courage to ask Becky to the movies – he can afford it. He opens messages and texts her, asking if she would like to go to the movies with him this afternoon.

Becky writes back with a 'YES'. Nick's little heart skips a beat; he's shy and was pacing his bedroom until she replied. Nick wants to pay for Becky to go to the movies seeing as he was the one that invited her; he doesn't want to pressure her into paying for herself.

Nick is nervous but he goes and tells his dad that he finally asked Becky to the movies and she said yes. His dad asks him if he had enough money to cover the two tickets and some snacks for them both. Nick nods excitedly and logs into his banking app to show his dad he has it covered. But then, Nick drops his phone; all his money is gone. Every cent – how could that be?

Can you guess what happened to poor

innocent Nick after reading about links?

When he received that text message with the unbelievably awesome win (which was a scam text), he clicked on the link and it installed a virus on his phone. That's what caused the screen to flicker (although it doesn't always cause that, it was a big giveaway!). This virus showed the bad person exactly what Nick was doing on his phone and what he typed where.

When he went home after he finished his paper route, he opened the banking app and entered his password – giving the bad girl or guy all his login information for his bank account. They then went in and transferred out his hard-earned money.

Poor Nick now has no money for his date (and must start from scratch for his future business), he needs to wipe his phone, reset his passwords and tell the bank about what happened. This might have all been avoided if he didn't click on that link.

We have a general rule and it's a little like this: If something looks too good to be true, it probably is.

So don't click on strange links on websites, text messages, emails – or from anyone you don't know. Still be careful about the people you do know because if their social media, phone or email has been taken over by bad guys or girls they could still be bad links.

Links are dangerous and should be always treated with caution no matter who they are from. If you think they are real and safe, pick up the phone or go talk to the person and ask them what it is before you click on the link. Also, remember from our chapters about anti-virus software, they can also help stop bad links from opening or bad executable files from downloading.

Remember, the more locks on the house, the less easy it is to rob! So, make sure your devices are in tip-top shape so people have less of a chance of tricking you into slipping into a shadow.

Group Questions

Question 1. Have you ever clicked on a link that has been bad before? What happened and what was it that made you click on it?

Question 2. If you saw a pop up ad that was trying to make you click on a link to take you to a website – what things would you ask yourself before you clicked it? What different things do you think could happen if you clicked that link?

Question 3. Why do you think people try to lure people in to fake websites? What do you think these malicious people could do with personal information?

It's Time to Go Shopping!

You can buy almost anything online; seriously, it's true.

You could buy a house or a car, doing everything online and never actually seeing it in real life before you own it. Most items you can buy and a few days later they will arrive at your door (that's even true with a car, but a house – maybe not so much!). There are huge websites like Amazon Prime where you can buy almost anything to be delivered the next day or websites like eBay where you can sell your old stuff or buy other people's things. There is no physical browsing, touching or looking at the quality of items, you just judge the quality by the look of the photos or reviews, maybe the quality of the website.

How we buy things has been changed forever

as the convenience and ease of access to anything we want will ensure that it only becomes a more common way of shopping in the future. With this new world and a new way to shop, we need you to consider a few shadows and how to light them up.

It may be an obvious one but remember when you are looking at buying something online, these things still cost real money. Your trusted adults will need to pay for whatever it is or you will need to pay with your own pocket money or after-school income. Make sure you have permission to buy something before you buy it. This goes for things like games from app stores as well as clothes or other cool stuff you see online.

You also need to really look at the website you are buying from – have you heard of them before?

Do they have physical stores you have been in before? How trustworthy is the site – is it possible that the site is a scam selling you 'too-good-to-be-true' bargains? You know what I mean, $1800 iPhones for $400 or a PlayStation for $150 – wow, that would be a great price if it were real but it won't be.

The best thing to do is research and luckily that is easy! Look up (through Google or another search engine) the reviews of that website and see if anyone else has bought from them before. If you are not sure, talk to your trusted adults about it; they can help you check them out before you buy, maybe protecting you from being scammed out of your hard-earned money!

Never put your bank card or bank information into a website before you have done your homework – make sure they are a good place to buy from first. A good idea for a first-time purchase on a new site is to make the purchase small – just buy one thing – and wait until you get that first item. If you are happy with what you get and the service, then you can buy more things from them if you like. This way, you have minimised your risks and have been able to firsthand validate the store.

A lot of shops online use photo-editing software to make things look a lot better than they do in real life, so reviews and triple checking is the best way to stay happy! There are payment methods such as PayPal that also make life easier by being the payment in-between you and the store you're buying from. So, you have a PayPal account that uses your bank card and you then pay for the item using PayPal as the payment method – meaning the site never has access to your bank card details. This means that if anything goes wrong, you can raise a complaint with PayPal, who has your back. If you never get the item, or if the item is not what it should be, you may even get a refund if PayPal agrees with you.

So, enjoy the amazing flexibility and convenience of the digital shopping world but remember to be careful, consider your risks and make smart choices. When online shopping, shine that torch of knowledge into every single pocket of a jacket before you buy it, every curve of a gaming console or every line of a piece of art. Check reviews, check measurements and dimensions – because, with photo angles and editing available these days, you may think you're buying a real horse and then a toy one turns up in the mail!

Group Questions

Question 1. What is your favourite thing to shop for online, or if you haven't yet, what are you looking forward to shopping for online the most? Why?

Question 2. What can you do if you fall victim to a fake online store? Who at the bank could you call to chat to about this? What are some ways you could protect yourself?

Question 3. Do you buy from stores online that you don't know? Do you do some research on the site before buying? Why do you think it's important to check before you checkout?

I Messed Up! What Do I Do?

Learning how to navigate the digital world is not an easy task; you will make mistakes, some small ones and probably some big ones. Some will cost nothing, some might cost money, some might cost pride – but I want you to know that it's okay and it's normal to make these mistakes.

If we learn from the mistakes we make and we communicate clearly about our mistakes with trusted adults, everything will be okay. That's how we become awesome adults and how one day you may have the life skills and knowledge to write your own book teaching other people about how to watch out for what lurks in shadows! It's through handling our mistakes that we learn.

Think about when we learned to walk. For

those who have been gifted with that ability, we start out sliding over the floors as babies, dragging ourselves from place to place and then we upgrade to crawling, which is faster and helps build our strength. Then we start to pull ourselves up on things, starting to stand up, before one day we decide to let go, take that first step out into the open and walk without help for the first time. Yes, we might fall a few times (well, probably more than just a few) but now we can run, we can jump and climb and play and we don't even think twice about it.

Those bumps and bruises from your falls are all part of a learning process. It teaches us what works and what doesn't, how to do things better and how to succeed. We get stronger at whatever we are trying to do through this process. Yes, we might get upset and hurt sometimes when we fall but that's okay if we pick ourselves up and do it again and again until we perfect it.

I want you to think of the digital world like this experience of learning to walk. Mistakes will happen, that is certain. Don't be ashamed of it, don't hide them and talk to your trusted adults about what happened (or better yet, have those conversations before they happen – use this book to start a conversation). You can fix those mistakes together – or seek help from your computer store or police station and learn from what happened. Use these mistakes to make yourself a better digital user. You will become more confident, more secure and able to know when to ask for help.

If you fell over as a toddler and then just decided to give up trying to walk, what sort of life would that be? The same goes with these digital life challenges and finding what's in the cyber shadows. You will likely mess up or even fail at the start of many journeys in life but what we should do is train ourselves and build up our skills until we win and we nail that challenge. If you have the desire to succeed, you will. It might cost you some time, effort and pride and you may get a few wobbles and falls along the way but you will be a better person for it.

Asking for help isn't always easy, we know that. A common human trait is to think we know best; we don't like to admit we have flaws or weaknesses but we all have them. Let's embrace them with confidence; let's be open about all of it. If you can be honest and talk openly with your trusted adults, your friends and your family about your mistakes in the digital space, it will help you and them. This is about helping you learn to navigate the internet and the ever-invading digital world and to help us come out stronger on the other side, becoming a confident superhero of the digital world. Don't let pride or being shy get in the way of you problem-solving and winning fights against cyber villains or bullies.

In life, if you fall nine times and get up ten, people will only remember the time you got up because that is what matters. Never be shy or embarrassed to mess up or fail because it means you had the confidence to try at the start – and I'm sure, dear reader, you will have the confidence to train, build, get back up and stand up strong.

Always remember, even superheroes need help sometimes.

Group Questions

Question 1. Have you ever made a mistake online, clicked on a fake link, installed a malicious app, or just gone somewhere you shouldn't have? Or have you heard a story from a friend who has? What happened?

Question 2. Do you feel comfortable telling your trusted adult or teachers when you make a mistake online? Do you know the phone number of your local police station in case you need to go to them first?

Question 3. Is it better to admit something went wrong or should you hide it?

Staying Mentally Healthy Online

This is a very important topic we think we all need to talk about more. Not just now but often.

We really want you to read this chapter and think about it, and then go start conversations about it with your teachers, your trusted adults and your friends. We want it to be something you all keep talking about as openly as we do in the cybersecurity industry.

Mental health is a complicated topic but it basically means your mind, your thoughts and how you feel – happy, sad, nervous or scared. Sometimes in this digital world we live in, we don't get the human interaction we need and we can start to feel a little isolated and disconnected from the world around us.

When we spend a lot of time online, we can

start to think everything we see is real and normal – like pictures of people your age, how they look and what people consider attractive or desirable. It's very important to remember even the people you see in those pictures usually don't look like that in real life! Photo-editing software is very common and easy to use, so much so that if you see celebrities in real life sometimes you can't even recognise them at the start. So, try not to judge yourself against others online as it can make you feel sad, or miserable, you may even start not liking things about yourself. I know this is hard to do but what makes you different is what makes you unique, it makes you!

This is only going to become more common as we dive deeper into the digital world and start to do more in that space than in our real world. We want you to do something that will help you be healthier mentally and feel more a part of the real world. Remember to disconnect from the digital world, go outside and enjoy some fresh air and playtime with friends face to face, playing sports, riding horses or even just playing catch.

Yes, gaming is fun, we get it and we agree! But

we need to just pull that plug sometimes and get away from the screens, enjoy nature instead and form real-life connections with the people around us. You will find yourself thinking more clearly and be happier for it. Don't get sucked into an online void way of thinking or be swept up in what others are saying online – step away, take a big breath and remember you are your own person with your own thoughts, feelings and opinions.

If you do feel down and like you need to talk to someone, there are a lot of people you can talk to. Your trusted adults, your friends, your friends' trusted adults, your teachers, counsellors, coaches, local police – so many! They will all listen if you need an ear, someone to talk to and think through your thoughts and if they're busy or they don't understand you, try another one. Problems are never as big as you think they are when you find someone to share them with.

Dealing with the online world can make people nervous or stressed out – even to the point of having a sore tummy, especially if bullies are giving them a hard time online. We never know what is happening at someone's home or what little comment might push them over the edge into being really sad – which is why we need to remember our bullying chapter and why even online we need to remember our words matter greatly.

If you are worried about what people will think if you tell them you are feeling down or stressed out, please don't be scared. Every single person in the world has times when they feel like that. If you don't feel comfortable telling your trusted adults when you're feeling sad or upset, if you have made a mistake or someone is trying to make you do something you don't want to do, luckily there are people you can call to discuss your feelings with and get advice from. There is the Kids Helpline, Beyond Blue, Your Town and many more platforms that you can reach out to for help. They are private, they won't tell your trusted adults if you don't want them to and they are free, so don't ever try to go through those sad times alone.

Sometimes the world needs to band together to help a superhero when they need it, so that same superhero can be in top mental health form when the world needs saving!

Group Questions

Question 1. How many hours per day do you think you are spending online? Do you think this is too many or too little?

Question 2. Do you disconnect sometimes, just go outside and get some fresh air? Why do you think this could be important to do as well as having fun online?

Question 3. Do you think about mental health and what spending too much time gaming or online does to your body and mind?
What are some negative effects spending too much time online could have do you think?
What are some positive effects spending time online could have?

The Superheroes of the Shadow World

Nearly everyone loves a movie superhero. They defend the world from villains and evil monsters and save the day. They save people's lives and do spectacular, super-human things. They protect the most vulnerable and they keep the world turning.

But there are some superheroes other than the ones on TV – ones that defend us every day. Ones that are fighting a secret battle to keep your lights on, to keep your family safe, to keep the grocery stores open, to keep our cities alive and everything (like our bank accounts, medical records, video streaming sites and social media sites) secure and working well.

These are the superheroes of the cyber world.

There are so many superheroes that have

an array of different skills. There are chatty, bubbly ones that help co-ordinate big plans and fly all over the world learning the best technologies to use in each situation and there are quiet, technical ones that implement the big plans – there are so many different types! Could you be one of them?

Cyber security superheroes can work in heaps of different areas and have different skills, like ethical hackers who see how they can get into different weak spots of a system, cyber security consultants who work on long-term strategies to make networks harder to get into, cyber security awareness advisors who teach people how to be safer online, hands-on technical people who implement the technologies into networks, all the way over to super cool areas like cryptography, artificial intelligence, privilege access management and identity governance, digital police work and 'incident response teams' (for when a cyber-attack happens) and so much more! So many big words, right? Don't let that put you off – the cyber security world is an achievable career for every single one of you, all you need is the desire to do it and a laptop with good

Wi-Fi to get started!

All our cyber security superheroes play a part in keeping our digital worlds safe from criminals and bullies that want to disrupt and cause havoc in our lives. Sometimes these meanies do what they do for money, sometimes it is out of hate or just because they are not very nice people but we can rest assured that there are thousands upon thousands of cyber heroes out there day and night fighting this battle for us.

Cyber warfare is a scary word but one that is used often nowadays. Going to war doesn't just mean soldiers and ammunition anymore – it can mean that the opposing side is hacking into important government documents and exposing top-secret things, or they could be diverting sewage water into fresh water, meaning no one can drink anything but toilet water. Yuck, right? All these things can happen if our cyber security superheroes aren't there.

This chapter is not only to say thank you to these amazing people out there right now on the front lines of the cyber battle but to say to you, our dear reader: now that you have dived into this amazing world of cyber security and charged up your cyber knowledge torch, maybe you could use your cyber torch to light up some career pathways and join our cyber team in years to come. Maybe you could have a career as a cyber security professional. Maybe, just maybe, you could save the day for humanity!

It does sound cool, doesn't it – to be that superhero, to save the day? We want you in the cyber security or IT industry. Every gender, every age, every ethnicity – we need you to help us fight the good fight.

So, think about it, it is an interesting and challenging career that you might love. There's a job for every personality, whether you're chatty or quiet, technical, or non-technical, if you like being the star of the show, or the secret superhero saving the day from the shadows – there's a career avenue for you as a cyber security superhero.

Every day cybercriminals are getting smarter but so are we... with your help.

Come join us and let's save the world together.

Group Questions

Question 1. If you could have any job at all in the IT world, what would it be and why?

Question 2. If you could use technology to solve something in the world, what would it be? Things like world hunger, or homelessness – big problems. How do you think technology could help?

Question 3. Can you imagine a world where the internet just turned off? What do you think would happen? Would rivers stop running and lights stop working? Why?

Question 4. What do you think the most important thing you have learnt in this book was? Why?

The Back Matter

Let's dig a little deeper into a few meanings so that you can understand and learn more about some of these important topics. If you come across a word in any chapter of the book that you're unfamiliar with, we will try to help you learn more here. These will build on the provided group discussion questions after each chapter and will help readers get a better understanding of the content in this book but also the online world.

You will also find a list of useful resources that can help expand on what we have all learnt together.

Word Breakdown

Internet
The internet is a network that has been created to connect the digital space world to allow us all to interact and communicate instantly at almost any time with almost anyone around the world. It allows us to have virtual meetings via Teams or Zoom. We can send emails or messages to people on the other side of the world in just seconds, breaking down the barriers of distance.

Network
A network is multiple machines or devices that have been connected via either a physical network cable and a switch or via Wi-Fi or wireless network. It allows people who are on the network to share and interact. It can allow a computer to print to a printer on the network.

It can allow devices to connect to the outside internet connection that can be used to get emails, send messages and stream movies on platforms like Stan or Netflix. Networks connect you to your home, school, or work environments and beyond via the internet connection.

Satellite

A satellite is a device that has been launched into space and has been placed in the Earth's orbit. It will float around in space, circling at a similar height from the Earth's surface, allowing our devices to connect to it. This can allow devices to access the internet or a private network such as military or telecommunications to allow phone calls or other types of access.

Virtual

Virtual is a digital version of the real world; it can refer to meetings through Teams or Zoom. It would be a virtual world inside a virtual reality space like the metaverse being built by Facebook, which will be accessible with virtual reality headsets or in other forms as the technology develops. It is not the real world; it cannot be physically touched, only interacted with in a digital sense.

Social media

Social media is a platform such as Facebook, TikTok, Instagram, LinkedIn and many more where users of the platform can interact with friends in a virtual sense through things like text content or images. Users of these platforms can comment and message other members of the platform. They are spaces put together to allow users to stay connected with people they follow. It has been a very successful introduction into modern-day society with many of the world's population taking part in various forms.

Facebook

Facebook is a website that was founded by Mark Zuckerberg. It is one of the most successful social media platforms and is essentially both a website and an app that allows users to message and interact with others and share posts with their friends. It allows text, video and pictures to be shared, as well as links to other websites.

TikTok

TikTok is a video-sharing platform that has generated a large user base, mostly teenagers sharing dance routines or silly videos with their friends and the world. Many businesses and other media personalities have been building a strong follower base. Videos can be captioned and shared and can be commented on. But trolling is popular on TikTok which can be quite negative.

Downloads

What is a download? Let's say you are on a website like Apple Books or an online bookstore. You have been wanting new books from some amazing authors – Craig Ford and Caity Randall. They are doing cool things. You find their latest book in digital form and go through the process of buying it from the indie bookshop. The payment finishes and you receive a link via email for you to retrieve your new book.

Very exciting, I know. You click the link, it starts to pull that file down from the indie store' online storage and within a few minutes, the book is on your computer. Guess what, you just downloaded the book. When you clicked the link and it started to pull the file from its online storage location, this is called downloading. This is the same if you download applications or files.

Apps

What is an app? Well, firstly 'apps' is just a shortened name for applications. It is the software you use to read emails, it could be a game that you play on your phone or your computer, or it could be a cloud file storage location. These are all applications that are used to perform certain functions or activities that you need them to do. Some apps can be very big like Microsoft Office, or small like a new drive on your computer to help it run properly.

Google

Google is a search engine that allows you as a user to go to and type in a few keywords of something that you want to buy, find, or just look at on the internet. In the background, it will have already trawled the internet looking for every detail about every website and it uses that information to help match what you are looking for with what it has seen. Google is one of the most popular search engines available to you as an internet user.

Google, over time, has become more than just a search engine but it is still one of its primary functions.

Malicious site

A malicious site is a website that has been created to infect your computer or device with some form of virus. It is a site made by a cybercriminal or malicious actor to gain some sort of advantage or to help them scam you out of your hard-earned money.

Virus

A virus in a computer sense is a malicious application that has been created to infect and help spread either a malicious payload to gain access to your computer systems or to spread ransomware. It is normally delivered via a malicious website; a file that is being used by malicious actors (bad people) to try and break through your device's security.

Trojan horse

A trojan horse in the computer world is when an application has been made to look and feel like it is useful to the person who is downloading and installing it on their devices. It still could be useful but it would hide a sinister and malicious application within that will execute during the initial install or at a set time later.

Android

This is a platform created by Google to run on mobile devices. It allows users to install and run the devices and purchase apps or content via the Google marketplace. It is the primary platform in competition with Apple and its iOS platform.

Apple

Apple is the maker of the Apple iPhone and Mac computer range. It runs its own proprietary operating systems or software. It also has its own marketplace to enable it to sell music, books, applications and much more. They are also one of the most valuable companies in the world at the time of writing this.

Windows

This is an operating system that most of you will use on any generic PC or laptop. It's the primary operating system used in most computers or most organisations around the world. It is the base platform on which you will install your applications like Word or Outlook.

Online marketplace

An online marketplace is a website or online store where you can buy digital products from the Apple store, Google Play and others. They are where you get games or books or music and more from for your devices.

Computer bugs

This term is used interchangeably on occasion with a virus but there are two real definitions of this in the context of computers or electronic devices. Yes, the first one is that it could be a computer virus that is an application designed to infect or damage a device. The second is a bug in a computer code, an issue that was made mistakenly or just accidental and is not an intentional issue or action. It can do damaging things to a system or application, or it can just cause it to do something unexpected like crash or give a strange response.

Website

A website is a location on the internet that holds a set of digital assets that you as a visitor can go to, so you can learn more about the owner of the site which could be an individual, a company or community group and so on.

Online gaming

Online gaming is a form of gaming, like how you would play on a computer or your Xbox or PlayStation. It could be a strategy game, virtual card game or almost any game that you can play against other opponents. You would open up the game on your device (this is also possible on Xbox or PlayStation) and you would connect to the online game option. It would normally connect you up to the game's online platform which allows you to either join current games being played or to start a new online session that others can join in with you. You can sometimes select who you would like to invite to these games or you could make it open for anyone to connect.

Online gaming is becoming quite a common way of gaming but it is also an easy way for malicious actors to connect with random people, build fake relationships with other players and to help them scam you in some way. They can do this either via a game mod that is a virus, getting you to click on links or just by giving out personal information to them when you shouldn't. This is normally done easily via the inbuilt chat functions in these games.

Online forum/community space

These spaces are normally topically-related spaces where like-minded individuals who are interested in the same topic or game, or movies, can go and write messages or posts that others in the group can see and interact with.

They are designed to build a community or strong fan base location for a brand or product. This will allow users to discuss and self-promote with each other. It is very common in gaming and other related communities.

Chat

Chat is something you will find on many websites and gaming forums. It is a live text-based instant communication method that allows staff from the website's company to directly answer questions or help with sales enquiries. It is an easy and cost-effective way to help boost customer satisfaction and sales.

It is also a common method of communication for online games or user forums. It should be noted that you should always be a little suspicious of chat communications and don't give out personal information to anyone on these sessions unless you trust the site one hundred per cent. If you didn't go to the website and initiate the conversation, then don't trust the source.

Email

Most people have used email in some form, it could be in Outlook or through an online website mail client in Google or Office 365. It is a text-based form of a digital letter platform. It is a way to send files and pictures to contacts via their email address. Emails can be replied to and you can keep a trail of communication.

Emails are one of the most common forms of communication in businesses today. Chat is becoming a bigger component of internal communications for quick easy statements or instant conversations but email will still be the main digital communication medium for many more years to come.

Link

A link is essentially an address for an online location. It could be to download a file, take you to a movie or website, or maybe even buy a book online like this one. It would normally consist of these components:

The initial HTTPS:// or HTTP:// is the indication that it is a site using the hypertext transfer protocol but it's the S or no S that is more important. If it has an S, it is using SSL security encryption on the site's location and is a safer form of a site. It's not a guarantee that the site is safe but is the better of the two options for encrypted communications with the location on or not encrypted.

The next section would normally be www, which just stands for the world wide web. It isn't always there or required. You could then have a subdomain like https://docs or https://www.docs or something along those lines. Next, you would go to the company's domain like the one for Craig's author site: craigfordauthor.com. This could also be anything like google.com.au or cyberunicorns.com.au.

So, what could it look like together?
https://theshadowworld.com.au/ or
https://www.google.com.au or
https://craigfordauthor.com/

These are all links and you will start to learn how to read them better the more you see and use them. A point of warning though, don't just go and click on random links, be cautious and only click on links that you know are safe or you have verified with who sent them to you first.

It could have a virus waiting for you at the other end of that click, so be safe.

Ransomware

This is a form of a virus that in recent years has been causing big problems for many businesses and organisations around the world. It infects your computer systems and spreads through to any other connected systems before executing the task of encrypting and locking down all your files. That means your emails, your pictures, your documents and everything else on the computer. It encrypts everything and will then normally display a ransom note on the device screen telling the victim they need to pay a ransom in cryptocurrency.

Encrypted

Essentially, encrypted means that the file has been locked or secured using a form of cryptography to change and secure a file or files with a special key, which is then able to be used to unlock the files. It is something that is done by individuals who want to ensure that files are secure and private but it is also a process used with ransomware viruses to ensure that system owners pay the bad people to get files back.

Scam

A scam is a situation when someone is trying to mislead you/someone into thinking they are getting something of value to them but they are actually trying to mislead, aiming to get something from the target like money, information, or something of value they need.

Phishing

Phishing is when a malicious actor emails a bulk set of emails with a generic email urgently asking you to do something, give them your bank details, send them Visa gift cards, click on a link, or go to a site so they can get access to your systems or steal your login information or just steal your money.

Remote access

This is when you connect via a computer or device to a system that is in another physical location. It could be your office computer sitting on your desk, or it could be a server that is sitting in the cloud that you are using to do your work from, to enable you to work from anywhere in the world.

Computer

A computer is an electronic device that has been created to allow a user to run software and do actions or activities. It allows a user to interact with the digital world through websites or even gaming.

Malicious actor

A malicious actor is a bad person in the context of the cyber world; they could be referred to as a cybercriminal or even just a criminal. This is someone that is using a digital world or digital systems to do malicious things to companies or individuals.

They are sometimes mistakenly named hackers but being a hacker does not make you a bad guy or girl.

Hacker

Let's start with what a hacker is not. A hacker is not the hooded figure sitting in a dark room breaking into all your computers; they are not all bad people or criminals stealing your information. Those bad people you are thinking of are better called cybercriminals, malicious actors or even just criminals.

A hacker is a person who has the innate

curiosity to manipulate things to do something they may not have been designed to do, to pull things apart and see what they can do with them and then put them back together. They are the cyber scientists who are here to help defend the cyber world from those bad people. They are the superheroes of this story, not the villains.

Online

What does online mean? Well, the simplest answer is when you are looking at something or doing something on the internet. The internet is the area that is referred to as online. It is the world that lives on the internet with games and websites.

Password

A password is a secret that you type into a computer or website to log in. It can be a combination of numbers and letters or even symbols.

PDF

PDF stands for Portable Document Format and is essentially the format of a document that is associated primarily with Adobe and is used to share contracts or printed and scanned documents via email or other electronic means.

Cybercriminal

A cybercriminal is a person who uses the internet to conduct criminal activities. It could be hacking into computers, it could be selling illegal content online, or even people who try to scam victims out of money or take over their accounts online.

Pop-up

A pop-up is a window that comes up away from the main window you are using while searching the internet or browsing a website. It will normally be some kind of ad relating to the current site you are looking at or it can be a malicious window trying to get you to approve an action for them to infect your systems.

Online banking

Online banking is when you go onto a browser on the internet and go to your bank's website, log in with your credentials and then you can access your bank account. You can look at how much money you have in the bank, pay bills or transfer money to someone else's account.

Cyberbully

A cyberbully is a person who belittles or harasses someone online. They could act exactly as a bully does in the real world: call someone names, say horrible or false things about a person and make someone feel horrible about themselves. The difference between a cyberbully and a bully (who can be the same person) is that the cyberbully can inflict pain on the victim at any time of day they want. There is no escaping them, they can do it whether the victim sees it or not and embarrass them continuously.

Internet/online troll

What is a troll as far as online and, on the internet, goes? Well, it is not a mythical creature that hides out under a bridge to jump out and scare travellers who try to cross their bridge. Although, what they do is probably just as bad. A troll in the online sense is someone who, for no real reason, will go to online posts or content and go out of their way to give horrible and sometimes defamatory feedback or comments. They will go after on occasion one particular person, who, for whatever reason, they have generated a disliking to and they will insult them in any way they can and will even threaten them physically in some instances.

There have been many cases in which online trolls ruin people's lives and businesses. People feel that because the trolls are online, they can do or say anything but that is not the case. In Australia, the act of trolling can be held liable and receive massive fines or even jail time. Everyone should consider that what they say online could hurt the person or business they are saying these things about. Is it valid or do they have the truth? We all need to act as we would in real life – don't be keyboard warriors and become online trolls.

Cloud storage
Cloud storage is a virtual storage area hosted for you or your organisation in the cloud. It could be through Azure, AWS, Google or even Cryptoloc. It is essentially the same as the storage you hold in your laptop or computer but it is provided to you by one of these suppliers and you are charged a fee to keep your data. It is secured for you via login information as you would have on local computer systems.

GPS

Global Positioning Systems or GPS for short are satellite tracking or navigation systems that we all commonly use to help us firstly pinpoint locations across the Earth. It could be used to place position markers for mapping or just to track where our fleet of company vehicles is located.

Many of us use it to get directions from point A to point B when travelling. It can help us find a business or coffee shop. It has essentially removed the need to carry or use paper maps as you would see in old movies such as National Lampoon's Vacation. We used to have to unfold massive pages and try to follow the impossibly complicated physical maps, trying to ensure you knew where you were and have the map the right way up, so you don't get your wires crossed and get completely lost.

Device

A device could be either a mobile phone, a laptop, a tablet, or something along those lines. It is something that we use to access the internet, emails, or music. They are becoming more and more powerful every day. The need for a desktop device is reducing all the time because the capability of cloud services is becoming very easy.

Install

To install something is when you go to an online store or marketplace on your computer or device and then click download or install on the chosen app or game. It will then run a process which is called installing to allow it to be available on your device. Once you have finished the install processes, it will have been installed on your device and you will be able to find the application or game on your device. If you click the icon, it will allow you to open the chosen application.

IoT

What is IoT? It stands for the Internet of Things. It refers to anything that is connected to the internet and can allow you to either collect information from it or control it via the internet or a local network. It can be smart lights that allow you to control them via an app on your mobile devices. For example, you could dim them, or turn them on or off. Maybe it could be an air conditioner that allows you to turn on the heating or cooling while you are not home to get your home to a comfortable temperature before you arrive. It could be a smart roller door that can tell you if you forgot to close it when you left in a hurry this morning and allow you to close it remotely.

There are many options and an ever-growing number of devices and use cases for IoT but this will give you an idea of what the word means.

Mobile device
A mobile device is a mobile phone or tablet or even a laptop. It is a reference to a device that is easily portable and can be used to connect to the internet or allow access to some sort of app. These could be for work or entertainment purposes. Most people have some form of a mobile device in today's age and they are becoming big parts of how we interact as a society.

Online portal
An online portal is normally a website that allows you to go and enter some credentials with a secret password as a minimum to authenticate yourself. It can provide you access to online banking, work documents, systems,

or even your children's school reports. They are becoming more common all the time and are now a primary method for organisations to share information with people easily.

The users are authenticated, they can track access and it can be very convenient for the users and the organisations who own the online portal.

Passcode

A passcode is a secret pin normally for a mobile device like a tablet or mobile phone. It is usually a numeric secret code to allow you to access the device. It is normally what is prompted when trying to unlock the devices and modern devices are sometimes replaced or complemented by either facial or fingerprint recognition. It ensures that only authorised people can access your devices, meaning if it is stolen or lost it is very difficult for anyone else to gain access to them.

The dark web

The dark web is a mysterious and dangerous place where you could see unicorns or goblins hiding. It's the underbelly of the internet where only the bravest ever venture. Okay, so you won't actually see unicorns or goblins unless it's pictured but it is the underbelly of the internet. It's not indexed by search engines because it is the playground of cyber criminals and hackers alike.

It can be a place in which you can find almost anything but it is a dangerous place that we would recommend you stay away from unless you are a trained professional. You don't want a criminal turning up at your home in real life because of something you do on the dark web.

Tread carefully here, it is not somewhere that is forgiving.

Online store

An online store is a website on the internet that you can go to and buy something. It could be a book like this, or food or clothes or honestly almost anything today. If you can buy it in a physical store, you will be able to find an online store that will also sell it.

You will be able to pay for what you buy by credit card, direct deposit or one of the many online payment platforms.

PayPal/Afterpay

These platforms are called payment gateways for payment providers like Mastercard or Visa. They are used in the online world through online stores or online marketplaces to enable their customers to buy through those locations. They are the middleman of the transactions, helping protect their customers from fraudulent transactions and ensuring a customer can get their money back if the store doesn't provide the goods as required from the purchase.

Disconnect

This means you will drop off and no longer be connected to whatever it is that you have been connected to. This could be the internet or social media. It can occur because of a connectivity issue or by choice with the user disconnecting themselves as needed.

Handy Links and Resources

eSaftey Commissioner
https://www.esafety.gov.au/
On the eSafety Commissioner's site, you will find some great basic resources to help explain the best ways to approach situations and some risks. It gives some good content as a starting point. You can also contact eSafety if you are being threatened or taken advantage of online and they will help or can get you in contact with people who can.

IDCARE
https://www.idcare.org/
IDCARE is supporting individuals impacted by recent data breaches, victims of cyber-financial crime and romance scams.

Life Education

https://lifeeducationqld.org.au/our-programs/primary-program/bcyberwise/

Kids Helpline

https://kidshelpline.com.au/

Kids Helpline is for more than just cyber safety and is a great organisation that is available for kids to call and talk to if they feel the need, to talk about bullying, mental health, or anything they need.

Author's Websites:

https://theshadowworld.com.au or
https://craigfordauthor.com

About the Authors

CAITY RANDALL

Caity Randall is a passionate individual who has strong philanthropic interests and believes with the one life we have been gifted, we should be using it to leave lasting positive impacts on the world. With years of experience and real-world knowledge of the cyber security industry, she has identified that there is a large gap in cyber education and awareness in both the younger generation plus their teachers and guardians.

Combining her experiences with her entrepreneurial spirit, author Caity Randall aims to educate and raise awareness surrounding sensitive cyber security and online safety topics in a palatable way for both schools and families with young children.

The 2022 finalist of "The One to Watch in IT Security" award, Caity is a strong voice within the IT industry and strives to be the written voice to empower kids to avoid the shadowy corners of the online world - or if they end up in them, to have the confidence to know they are not alone and how to reach out for help.

DEDICATION

This book is dedicated to my past self who struggled heavily with who and what to trust online – and the trauma and stress that I went through when I made the wrong choices out of naivety.

ACKNOWLEDGEMENT

Thank you to Bev Randall – who is always my life cheerleader and sounding board, without you this book wouldn't be a reality.

CRAIG FORD

Craig is a cybersecurity engineer and ethical hacker. He has a Master's in Management (Information Technology) and a Master's in Information Systems Security from Charles Sturt University. He was awarded the AISA (Australian Information Security Association) Cyber Security Professional of the Year 2020 and was elected AISA Queensland Branch Chair in 2021.

Craig is a freelance cybersecurity journalist who is best known for his work on CSO Australia in which he contributed almost 100 cybersecurity articles between 2018-2020. He is a regular columnist for "Women in Security" Magazine and has contributed to the project since its inception in early 2021. He also contributes to Cyber Today, Cyber Australia, Top Cyber News and Careers with STEM magazines.

Craig has three previous books, two in the

A Hacker I Am series "A Hacker, I Am" and "A Hacker, I Am – Vol 2" which were self-published, these are cybersecurity awareness books which try and help educate everyone on how to be safer in this connected world. As well as Foresight, a cyberpunk, cyber espionage book published through Cyber Unicorns.

DEDICATION

I would like to dedicate this book to my children, my inspiration to want to help keep children safe in this digital world we all live in. With this book, I will be able to help not only keep you safe but help change the course for the next generation. Providing cyber education and awareness that will stay with you all for the rest of your lives.

COVER ILLUSTRATION CREATED BY
MICHELLE WEBB

Michelle is an artist/illustrator living on Mornington Peninsula. Combining her background in Fine Art with the latest in technology, she paints digital pieces that have a traditional feel to them... some so realistic that even her framers were surprised to feel no residue when handling her work.

Michelle is inspired by her own life experiences, music, mythology, culture, and nature in all its beauty, both light & dark. Her work ranges from stylised high fantasy to realistic portraiture, and she is at her happiest when combining fantasy with reality. While very new to this industry, Michelle is already making her mark and was honoured to be titled as a Painter Master by Corel Software in 2018, joining a prestigious line up of the most talented artists in digital.

INTERNAL ILLUSTRATIONS CREATED BY
M. K. PERRING

Growing up in England I loved reading and drawing! I was inspired by Roald Dahl, especially my favourite of his books 'The Witches', to keep making creative stories and drawing interesting characters. Moving to Australia was a huge cultural shift for me, but I made new friends and kept being creative. I didn't always know what to pursue in life, but I had to create, I loved art. I studied films, animation, graphic design and illustrations. I became a jack of all trades! It wasn't easy to follow my dreams, but I stayed positive, believed in myself, and listen to those who believed in me too. Now, making beautiful illustrations and working with all kinds of authors is a dream come true, and only the start of my adventure.

aisa.org.au

As a nationally recognised peak body for cyber security professionals, the Australian Information Security Association (AISA) champions the development of a robust information security sector by building the capacity of professionals, advancing the cyber security and safety of the Australian public as well as businesses and governments.

Established in 1999, AISA has become the peak body and think tank on information security in Australia with a membership of over 10,000 individuals and corporate sponsors across the country. AISA caters to all domains of the information security industry with a particular focus on sharing expertise from the field at meetings, focus groups and networking opportunities around Australia.

AISA's vision is for a world where all people, businesses and governments are educated about the risks and dangers of cyber attack and data theft, and to enable them to take all reasonable precautions to protect themselves.

Our independent non-profit association was created to provide leadership for the development, promotion, and improvement of our profession. Our strategic plan calls for continued work in the areas of advocacy, diversity, education, and organisational excellence.

www.aisa.org.au

www.ingramcontent.com/pod-product-compliance
Lightning Source LLC
Chambersburg PA
CBHW050224100526
44585CB00017BA/1893